The Poor Man's Prepping Guide: How to Prepare for Disaster on a Shoestring Budget

by M. Anderson

Disclaimer:

The information contained in this book is for general information purposes only. The statements contained herein have not been evaluated nor approved by the US Food and Drug Administration. This book is sold with the understanding the author and/or publisher is not giving medical advice, nor should the information contained in this book replace medical advice, nor is it intended to diagnose or treat any disease, illness or other medical condition.

While we endeavor to keep the information up to date and correct, we make no representations or warranties of any kind, express or implied, about the completeness, accuracy, reliability, suitability or availability with respect to the book or the information, products, services, or related graphics contained book for any purpose. Any reliance you place on such information is therefore strictly at your own risk.

Dedication:

This book is dedicated to my loving wife, who's had to deal with my obsession with backyard chickens, survival skills and homesteading for many long years. I love you sweetie! Thanks for being so understanding.

Contents

Will You Be Ready?

I want you to take a few minutes to assess how prepared you would be if a disaster struck at this very moment. If ten minutes from now a disaster strikes that completely cuts you off from the food, water and amenities you're used to, how prepared will you be?

Most people would be caught completely off-guard.

A large number of people don't have any of the supplies they would need to survive. These are the people you see on TV news reports crying about how the government left them without food and water for days on end when disasters like Hurricane Katrina hit with full force. They think that because they're citizens of America, they're entitled to food and water any time they want it.

"I sat there for six days and starved and no one came to help," said a lady on a recent newscast I watched. "The government didn't send nobody. Six days, no food. I was fixing to starve to death."

If you're counting on government aid to bail you out, you'd better recognize how low you are on the totem pole.

Yes, whenever possible, the government will send in aid, but that aid may take days or even weeks to arrive—and when it does, it may be sorely lacking. And what happens if a doomsday event takes place that renders the government completely incapable of providing any sort of aid? Most of the unprepared will die, either from thirst, starvation or disease.

Sorry to be so blunt, but I want you to understand the risk of not being prepared. Your survival depends on how prepared you are. The better prepared you are, the better off you and your family will be in an emergency situation. If you have the right gear and the right training, you'll be much more likely to survive than the people who couldn't be bothered to prepare when times were good.

There are going to be those who dismiss preppers as nothing more than "paranoid freaks." They see us as obsessed human beings who distrust everyone around us, especially the government. While there are indeed some preppers who live in underground bunkers in the middle of nowhere wearing tin foil hats to keep the aliens from reading their minds, there are a growing number of normal individuals jumping on the prepping bandwagon.

These are normal people like you and me who have taken a good look at their lives and decided they don't want to count on someone else for survival. You wouldn't know it by looking at them, but you see people every day who have the knowledge and supplies they need to survive in the event of an emergency.

There are three types of people when it comes to emergency preparedness:

- **Those who survive because they're prepared.** These are the people who are ready should disaster strike and, while survival isn't guaranteed, they're the most likely group of people to survive.
- **Those who survive because of luck.** This group of people survives due to blind luck. They either stumble upon a cache of food and supplies or they meet someone who's prepared and is willing

to help. I don't know about you, but I don't want to depend on the kindness of other (or blind luck) when my life is on the line.

- **Victims.** These are the people who do not survive. Depending on the severity of the situation, there may be a lot of victims or the number of victims may be limited. The less prepared you are, the more likely you are to fall into this category.

If a disaster happened right now, which of these categories are you most likely to fall into? If you answered anything other than the first category, it's time to start prepping.

What You Need to Prepare For

"What do I need to prep for?"

I've been asked this question more times than I can count. The answer is both simple and extremely complicated.

The simple answer is:

You need to prepare for as many different scenarios as you can afford to.

Where it gets complicated is when you start looking at all of the thousands of possibilities.

You could spend millions of dollars prepping (and people have) and still not be prepared for a disaster when it strike. A million dollar state-of-the-art bunker isn't going to do you any good if disaster strikes while you're away from home. All the top-notch survival gear in the world won't do you any good if it isn't located where you can easily access it when you need to.

There are literally tens of thousands of potential emergency scenarios that could take place that run the gamut from minor emergencies requiring a day or two of supplies to world-shattering doomsday scenarios where the vast majority of the people on the planet don't survive and those who do are tasked with rebuilding civilization.

Natural disasters are probably the most likely thing you need to prepare for. Here's a sampling of some of the natural disasters that could strike:

- **Avalanche.**
- **Big storm.**
- **Drought.**
- **Earthquake.**
- **Extreme cold or heat.**
- **Fire.**
- **Flood.**
- **Heat wave.**
- **Hurricane.**
- **Landslide.**
- **Lightning storm.**
- **Meteor.**
- **Sink hole.**
- **Solar flare.**
- **Tornado.**
- **Tsunami.**
- **Volcano.**

In addition to natural disasters, we have to worry about our fellow man and their potential for destruction. Here's a small sampling of the man-made disasters that could occur:

- **War.**
- **Nuclear war.**
- **Biochemical attack.**
- **Disease.**

- **Dirty bomb.**
- **Poisoning of the water supply.**
- **Rioting.**
- **Crime wave.**
- **Lack of law.**
- **Martial law.**
- **Terrorist attack.**
- **Arson.**
- **Civil disorder.**
- **Extended power outage.**
- **Interruptions to the food supply.**
- **Lack of clean water.**
- **Industrial accident.**
- **Release of hazardous material.**
- **Interruptions to public transportation.**
- **Economic collapse.**
- **Zombies.**

Zombies?

Ok, maybe that one was a little far-fetched. I was just checking to see if you were still with me.

These examples are just a small sampling of the potential disasters that could take place. Many of these disasters are highly unlikely, but the chance of *something* happening during your lifetime that you're going to need to be prepared for is much higher. While you can't possibly prepare for every single situation that may arise, you can look at the list and slowly but surely prep for the most likely situations to take place.

Prepping is highly an individual task.

You should begin prepping for the situations you think are most likely to occur in the area where you live and prepare for them in a manner that suits you. Looking at the list of natural disasters, a person who lives in certain areas of California would want to prepare for earthquakes first. People living along the coast may want to prep for tsunamis first and then earthquakes. A person living on the opposite coast would probably forget about earthquake preparedness and start with getting ready for hurricanes or flooding due to massive storms. People in the mid-West may decide tornadoes are their biggest threat and place them at the top of their list.

The key to preparedness is to start with the most imminent dangers first and move on from there. If you live in Wyoming, it wouldn't make any sense to prepare for a tsunami. It would take one heck of a wave to make it into the Cowboy State. Wildfire, winter storm or e tornado preparedness would be smarter choices.

Preparedness Overlap

The good news is a lot of the prepping you do will overlap from one disaster to another. If you start off prepping for flooding and create a bug out bag, build up a food supply and prepare to harvest clean water, all of these items are able to be used in the event a different type of disaster strikes.

You aren't going to have to create a supply of goods for flooding and then completely start over when you move on to the next disaster on your list. The goods you bought to prepare for flooding will be able to be used for the other emergency situations on your list. As you prepare for more and more disasters, you'll find yourself having to purchase fewer items because you're able to check many of the items you already have off of the list.

There's going to be a significant upfront cost to get all of the main supplies you need, but this cost will lessen as you'll have many of the supplies needed for other emergencies.

This "preparedness overlap" will allow you to accelerate your preparedness as time passes. Even if something occurs that you hadn't begun preparing for, you're going to have at least some of the stuff you need to survive. You'll be much better off than the people who didn't bother to get ready at all and you'll have a better shot at survival.

Keeping the Cost of Prepping to Minimum

No matter how you look at it, emergency preparedness isn't cheap. You're going to need gear, food, water, shelter and protection, at a bare minimum, in order to survive.

How much you spend is up to you.

There are preppers who have spent large sums of money on the best gear money can buy, underground bunkers, thousands of pounds of food and vehicles capable of traversing the roughest terrain. You'd think these people are poised to survive anything and everything, and some of them are. Sadly, others have wasted large sums of money on stuff that isn't going to help them one bit in a real crisis situation.

A lot of the time, it seems like these people just throw money down the drain in the name of preparedness without stopping to look at what they're actually spending their money on. Just the other day, I read about a guy who owns property in the middle of nowhere in South America that he plans on bugging out to when SHTF (Stuff Hits the Fan). Oddly enough, he lives in America and has no real means of getting there. He wants to buy a boat he can use to sail there, but hasn't procured one yet. That sounds like putting the carriage ahead of the horse to me.

Spending money just to spend it isn't my thing.

I don't have unlimited resources to spend on prepping. Hell, I barely have enough cash to pay the bills, let alone to blow tens of thousands of dollars on stuff I don't need for situations that aren't likely to occur. Despite my limited financial resources, I've managed to build up a decent little cache of survival gear that I believe has me prepared for a large number of disasters.

The tips, techniques and supplies laid out in the rest of this book were chosen to give you the most bang for your buck. You're going to have to spend some money getting ready, but *The Poor Man's Prepping Guide* seeks to keep the money you spend to a minimum.

Whatever you do, don't skip preparing for disaster because you think you can't afford it. The truth is you can't afford not to be prepared. Look at your life and find other places you can cut corners to free up some money.

You can thank me later.

Tips to Help You Save Money on Prepping

Preparedness is expensive, but it doesn't have to break the bank. There are a number of things you can do to cut down your prepping costs. The tips in this chapter are designed to help you save money and get the most out of each and every dollar you spend.

Tip #1: Plan ahead and don't think you have to buy everything at once.

Buying all of the survival gear and supplies you're going to need in one fell swoop would bust all but the most robust of budgets. You don't have to take out a second mortgage on your house to prepare for disaster. In fact, gradually building up your cache of supplies can save you money.

When you buy everything at once, you're going to have to pay full price for a lot of the stuff you buy. You aren't going to be able to take advantage of any sales or deals other than the ones that are being offered right now. What this means is you'll pay top dollar for gear you could wait a little while to buy and sometimes get for as much as half off.

Wondering how you can save that much?

Check out the next tip.

Tip #2: Wait until the end of the season to buy gear.

If you buy cold weather gear at the beginning of winter or camping gear at the beginning of summer, you're going to have a tough time finding what you want for decent price. When you do find it, you're going to pay big bucks because stores raise the prices on the gear they know people are going to want at the time. These stores will offer sales on a few items to get you in the door. Everything else will be full price.

I'm of the opinion you should never pay full price for anything, unless you have a pressing need to own it. If you want a lightweight hiking backpack, the only good reason to go to the store and pay full price for one is if you have a hiking trip coming up and don't already own one. If not, you should wait for the end of season sales.

While waiting for sales can net you decent deals, waiting until the end of season clearance sales kick in can net you even bigger savings. At the end of each season, stores have to get rid of the stock they have on the shelves to make rooms for stuff for the upcoming season. Some stores sell the items they have left from the previous season at rock-bottom prices. I've purchased tents, sleeping bags and snow gear for less than half of what it was originally priced at.

Unless you feel you absolutely have to have something, wait until the end of the season to get the best deals. If you catch the right sales, you'll be able to buy twice as much stuff with the same amount of money.

Tip #3: Don't spend money on gear you'll never use.

This may sound like common sense, but you'd be surprised how many people don't follow this advice.

Look at the area you live and the area you plan on bugging out to if you have to make a quick escape and plan accordingly. Avoid spending money on items you don't need and won't ever use.

Snowshoes are a great idea if you live in (or may have to head to) an area that gets a significant amount of snow. Your money is better spent on other items if you live in the desert. Be smart about your purchases and you'll be able to stretch your money a lot further.

Tip #4: You don't always need the most expensive gear.

When you first start prepping for disaster, you're probably going to do a lot of searching for supplies that best fit your needs. You're going to start off with something basic in mind, like a plain old canvas tent. By the time you're done shopping around, you're going to be convinced you want an ultra-light trekking tent with carbon fiber tent poles and built-in satellite radio, GPS and PlayStation 3hookups.

Sure, you could break the bank and spend a lot of extra money buying high-end gear with all the bells and whistles. It would be nice to have the best gear money can buy, but let's face it . . . if you could afford that stuff, you probably wouldn't be reading this book. Instead of spending a small fortune on a single high-end item, you're going to be much better off (and better fitted overall) spreading that money out across a number of mid-range priced items. You'll get a lot more gear this way, and the mid-range priced stuff is usually of pretty good quality.

Tip# 5: Don't buy a ready-made kit.

There are ready-made survival kits out there that purport to have everything you're going to need in case disaster strikes. They run anywhere from a couple hundred dollars to a couple thousand dollars, depending on how big the kit is and how big of a sucker the sellers are looking for.

These kits fail on multiple levels.

For one, you can usually create a kit of your own that has better (or at least the same) quality of supplies for less money if you take advantage of sales. I've seen thousand dollar kits that contain gear I could put together for a couple hundred bucks—and the sad thing is people buy them. I've seen a number of reviews touting what a good deal these kits are. If I was as unscrupulous as the makers of these kits, I could make a small fortune off of them—and people would thank me for it.

The biggest reason these kits aren't all they're cracked up to be is they're not usually tailored to any specific type of disaster or a person's individual needs. They contain gear that's designed to work in all emergency situations, instead of specific situations. A kit designed to be used in just a flood will have different gear than one designed for a person hoping to survive being snowed in for months. The premade kits don't differentiate between emergencies and largely fail to prepare you for anything.

Before you go shopping for gear, sit down and write out a list of everything you think you're going to need. If you're still sold on buying an "all-in-one" survival kit or bug out bag, try to find one that has everything you've written down and nothing more or less in it. I'll bet you can't do it.

It's going to take a bit of extra effort on your part and a little shopping around, but you can prepare for survival for

less money than one of the more expensive kits will cost—
and you'll be better prepared for the emergencies most
likely to strike your area.

Tip #6: Make room in your budget for prepping.

Your prepping costs should be part of your monthly
budget. You do have a budget, don't you? If not, it's time to
start. That way, you'll know exactly how much money you
have to spend on prepping every month.

If you set aside a certain amount of money every
paycheck, you'll know exactly how long it's going to take
you to save up for the items you need. If you want a $500
ultra-light backpack and have $100 budgeted for prepping
every month, you know you have to save up and put away
your prepping money for 5 months in order to get it.

Creating a budget and monitoring it closely for a few
months will allow you to see exactly where your money is
going. If you think you can't afford the expense of
prepping, take a look at some of the things you're spending
money on right now to see if there's anywhere you could
tighten up. Cutting back on a few cups of coffee and a
monthly night out on the town can free up a significant
amount of money that could be spent on disaster
preparedness.

Tip #7: Ask for preparedness items for gifts.

Asking for preparedness items for gifts for Christmas
and birthdays will help you cut down on costs. The more
items other people give you, the less you'll have to buy. I

don't recommend asking Aunt Gertrude for a $500 GPS system (unless she's loaded), but you might be able to get her to pony up for a new compass, a camp stove or another inexpensive prep item.

This will also solve another problem—unwanted gifts.

You won't have to figure out something to do with that pastel colored turtleneck your grandmother always knits you or the tube socks your mother gives you every year. Ask for preparedness items and you'll always get something you need and want.

Tip #8: Don't wait until the last minute to get the stuff you need.

You know what disasters are most likely to strike the area where you live. You need to prepare for these disasters sooner rather than later. If you're in an area prone to large winter storms, hurricane or other disasters that strike frequently, you know the items you're going to need. Buy them ahead of time in order to save both time and money.

When there's a large storm brewing, forecasters often know about it a few days to a week or more ahead of time. It's all over the news and all of the people who waited until the last minute to prepare have to run to the store to get the supplies they need. Stores run out of stock quickly and raise prices on the stuff they do get in.

You can forget about sale prices. You're going to have to pay whatever prices the stores decide to mark their items up to . . . If you can find the items at all. If not, you're going to have to find the items you need on Craigslist or from another place where local resellers gather—and you're going to get scalped. Once stores run out, people sell their excess gear for double, triple or even quadruple the normal going rate for it. People pay these prices because they know they have to have these supplies.

You can actually make a bit of money if you plan ahead. If there are a couple huge snowstorms a year in your area, make a checklist of all the items you need and buy them in advance. When the forecast says one of these storms is coming through, head to the store and check to see which of the items on your list have sold out. The next time around you can buy a few extra of each of these items in advance when you find them on sell and then turn around and sell them on Craigslist yourself. I don't recommend ripping people off, but if you sell your items for less than what other people are selling them, you're still going to make a profit—and people will be more than happy to pay your inflated prices.

Tip #9: Keep the change.

This tip alone can be used to help you save a couple hundred dollars a year to put toward prepping costs. Instead of using your bank card to pay for everything, use cash for everything you buy. Take the cash you'd normally spend on groceries, snacks, gas and spending money and separate it out into envelopes. This will allow you to track exactly how much money you're spending and will go a long way toward making sure you don't overspend on any of these items.

Now, when you spend cash, take the change you get and put it away. The best way to do this is to empty your pockets into an empty water bottle at the end of each day.

Count out your coins a couple times a year and use the money you've saved toward any gear or supplies you've been wanting.

Tip #10: Start small and add to it as you go.

Rome wasn't built in a day. You won't be able to build your emergency supply up in a day either. Start small and add to your stock bit by bit as you find good deals. Shoot for a two week supply of everything you need first. Start buying the food, gear and supplies you need to make it for two weeks.

This will give you a good goal to shoot for at first. Two weeks' worth of supplies will give you a good start and will get you through most emergencies. You'll be able to relax and breathe easy knowing you can handle almost anything the world throws at you.

Once you've built up a two week supply of everything you need, you can move on to building up a larger supply. Next, shoot for a month's worth of supplies. Then two months. Then three. Before you know it, you'll have built up 6 months to a years' worth of supplies and your pocketbook won't seem lighter because you've done it gradually.

Finding the Best Deals on Gear

As a poor prepper, you're going to have to find the best deals around in order to get as much gear as you possibly can for each dollar spent. Saving a few bucks on an item frees up more money that can be spent on other items.

I'm of the opinion you should never pay full price for the items you need. No matter what you want, it's being sold somewhere out there for a discount. When it comes to finding deals, we have it much better than people did just a few short decades ago. Modern technology allows us to branch our searches for deals out across the entire country—and sometimes even the world.

If we can't find a good deal locally, we can turn to the Internet, where there's often much better deals available. Never buy an expensive item in a brick and mortar store without checking online first. I recently made this mistake with a GPS unit I found at Bass Pro Shops for what I thought was an amazing deal. It was being offered at a huge discount from its normal price. I snatched it up and was happy with my purchase . . . until my wife pointed out that it was for sale on the Internet for $40 less than what I paid for it.

Lesson learned. Now, I never buy an item without first checking to see how much it is online. Don't forget to factor in the shipping costs. A lot of online companies offer items for what seem like great prices and make up the difference with high shipping and handling costs. What ultimately matters is the total amount you pay for an item. Shipping and handling costs add up. When you buy items on the Internet, you may not have to pay tax (depending on the site you buy it from), so be sure to figure tax into the equation as well. I live in an area where there's a 9% sales tax on purchases. That means I get taxed $9.00 for every hundred bucks I spend. On expensive items, this can add up quickly.

I've found that budget prepping requires you to be flexible when it comes to the brand name you're purchasing. Instead of picking out the exact item and brand you want, you can more often than not get the best deal by choosing the type of item you want and then shopping around for the best deal on that type of item. An example of this would be deciding you want a survival knife and then looking around to find which manufacturer is offering the best price on their knives.

The more shopping you do on a shoestring budget, the better you'll get at it and the more likely you become to find the best deals. Here are a few places great bargains can be found:

Flea markets. Never pay the full asking price. You can almost always get a better deal if you ask.

Thrift stores. The busier stores rotate new stock onto their shelves all day, every day of the week. It helps if you know someone at the store who's willing to contact you if the type of items you're looking for come in. If not, check the shelves frequently because you never know what you're going to find.

Dollar stores. Keep an eye out for good deals on food and supplies.

Garage sales and estate sales. Both are great places to find good deals on gear that's like new. You can usually talk people down in price. Arrive early for the best deals and check out yard sales in upscale neighborhoods if you're looking for high-end gear that's hardly been used.

Surplus stores. Some surplus stores are better than others. If you find a surplus store that buys their items in bulk, they may be able to sell them to the public for less than what many of the other companies pay for them. It doesn't hurt to check.

Craigslist. You can search for deals in your city. If you don't find anything locally, expand your search to other nearby metro areas. It may be worth driving a ways to get a great deal on an expensive item.

Amazon. When all else fails, turn to Amazon. When I need an item and I can't wait around for it to go on sale, I've found Amazon regularly beats the prices of most other stores. They also offer free shipping on orders over $25.

Ebay. Watch for auctions with no minimum price and wait until they're about to close to place your bid. Make sure you only bid on quality items. Ebay is full of junk that will fall apart on you the first time you try to use it.

Closeouts. At least once a week, scan the closeouts section of all of your favorite websites. You never know what might pop up in there and this is where you're going to find some of the best deals.

Clearance racks. Always check the clearance racks at your favorite stores. You never know when a great deal is going to show up.

End of season sales. These sales are where you're going to find some of your best deals on prepping gear. Big retailers will often place items they have left at the end of a season on sale for deep discounts in order to make room on their shelves for the next season.

Going out of business sales. I've managed to take advantage of a handful of going out of business sales locally. I purchased a bunch of gear from a local Surplus store that went out of business for 60% off the lowest marked price.

Couponing the Poor Prepper Way

Most preppers probably change the channel when shows like "Extreme Couponing" come on. I know I used to. That is, until my wife started finding great deals on food and toiletries where she was able to purchase them for next to nothing.

This got the gears turning in my head.

If my wife was able to find great deals on food and household supplies, there's no reason I couldn't do the same in order to build up a stockpile of food. I watched an episode of one of those shows and was surprised by what I saw. The first thing that shocked me is how wasteful some of those people are. They buy stuff just to buy it, and have huge stockpiles of stuff they'll never in a thousand years use.

The second thing I saw changed my view of couponing forever. Many of these "extreme" couponers have huge stockpiles of food, all purchased for pennies on the dollar. They seek out the best deals and plan their trips meticulously, and many of them are able to buy cart after cart of food for a quarter (or less) of what it would normally cost them.

Some of these people take couponing to the extreme, treating it like a full-time job. It isn't uncommon for extreme couponers to spend 40+ hours a week clipping coupons and planning their next shopping excursion. While most sane people don't want to put in that much time to save cash, there are a handful of things you can learn from these couponers that'll save you cash.

I call it Poor Prepper Couponing, and while you won't get carts full of food for $20 a cart, you'll save a decent amount of money off what you'd normally pay.

First, I gather my coupons.

I ask everyone I know to save their coupon inserts for me. Most people don't bother clipping coupons and your friends and family should be more than happy to save them for you. I get coupons from my mom, my brother, my uncle, my niece, my neighbor and three of my friends (when they remember). I also get two Sunday papers delivered to my house. I'm not above snatching the coupon inserts out of newspapers I see at Starbucks, auto dealers and the break rooms at work. You can also find a number of good coupons online, both on store websites and on sites like Coupons.com.

This gives me at least ten inserts from which I can harvest coupons. I gather them all up and spend a half hour or so sorting out the coupons I find that are for items that would be great to add to my stockpile. Here's where my tactics differ from those of most extreme couponers. I sort the coupons out by the type of item they are, but I don't clip them. I just put them in folders and wait to see if any deals pop up on those items.

When I see a good sale price on an item I have coupons for, I clip the coupons out and use them on the item. This saves me the hassle of spending hours clipping coupons out that I never use. I used to do it the hard way, but soon realized I was wasting a lot of time clipping coupons I ended up tossing when they expired.

If you have ten coupons, you can buy ten items and use one coupon on each item. If you have a manufacturer's coupon and a store coupon, most stores will let you stack the coupons for even more savings. What this means is if you have a Buy One Get One Free store coupon and a $0.50 off manufacturer's coupon, you can use both coupons at the same time. You'll get $0.50 off the item you're buying and you'll get a free item. Learn to stack coupons and you'll build up your emergency stockpile in no time.

You can save even more money if there are any stores in your area that have double or even triple coupon days. On double days, the store doubles the value of any coupons you bring in. If you have a $0.75 off coupon, it becomes a $1.50 off coupon on a double day. Care to guess what triple days are? That's right, the value of your coupons triples on triple days. A $0.30 off coupon becomes a $0.90 coupon on triple days.

You can get great deals on toiletries and other household items if you learn how to take advantage of store rewards programs like those offered at CVS and Walgreens. It's kind of a hassle to keep up with the rewards and the "dollars" you get to spend toward other items expire quickly, so you need to really be on top of things to maximize your savings. To be honest with you, it can be more of a hassle than it's worth, but you can get items for free or for a few cents if you play your cards right, so it's worth at least looking into.

There are occasional deals out there where you can make money. This usually happens when you stack a couple coupons to get a low price on an item and then get reward dollars on top of the coupons.

Here's an example I recently took advantage of. Schick Hydro Silk razors (which my wife uses) were on sale at Target for $7.99 each when you buy two. I used a store coupon that gave me $5 off when I bought 2 and stacked two manufacturer's coupons that gave me $4 off of 1 razor. The total price at the register was $2.98, which is a great deal for two of these razors. Target had a deal going where I got back a $5 gift card for buying two razors, so I ended up making a couple bucks on the deal.

In essence, they paid me to buy their product. Can't beat that.

I'm all about getting the most bang for my buck, but I'm kind of lazy when it comes to checking ads and searching for coupons. Luckily, there are a number of people who aren't lazy and are more than happy to share the deals they find. There are websites that spoon-feed you the best deals and even tell you where you can get the coupons to take advantage of the deals.

You can take advantage of these people's kindness by checking the following websites a couple times a week:

http://www.cuckooforcoupondeals.com/

http://thekrazycouponlady.com/

http://hip2save.com/

http://www.couponmom.com

http://www.frugalcouponliving.com/

http://dealseekingmom.com/

http://www.creativecouponing.com/

http://www.totallytarget.com

Watch these sites closely for free samples being offered by manufacturers for free.

You can sometimes get trial size samples for free. All you have to do is enter your e-mail address into a web form and tell the manufacturer where to send the sample. Don't use your normal e-mail for this because your inbox will soon be full of spam. Set up a separate account that you only use for this purpose and you won't have to worry about sorting through hundreds of advertisements when you go to check your emails.

Keep an eye on the e-mails you're getting in this account. Sometimes manufacturers and stores will send out special coupons for the people on their mailing lists.

One warning about couponing.

Finding deals where you get stuff for free or almost free can get a bit addicting. You need to be careful not to get caught in the trap of buying stuff just to buy it because the price is right. You need to buy stuff that's going to add value to your stockpile. Clearing store shelves just because you can is selfish and will end up costing you more money in the long run.

Only buy what you need and you'll be much better off.

Making a List and Checking It Twice

Creating a list of all the items you need to purchase and the normal cost of each item will help you determine when you've found an item at a price you can't pass up. Sales come and go in cycles, with the lowest prices on each item rolling around once every three to six months.

When you first start prepping, you're going to have a lot of items on your buy list. Write down each of the items, the current lowest price you can find the item for and the date the item was added to the list. Keep an eye out for the items you want and watch how the prices fluctuate. You might be surprised at just how much the prices on the items you want move up and down throughout the year.

Watching an item fluctuate in price will allow you to determine the best price you're going to get an item at if it goes on sale. It also gives you the chance to recognize a hot deal when one rolls around. I was recently in the market for a gas-powered generator and used the watch-and-wait technique of checking prices. I waited 6 months and watched stores in my local area to see if the generator ever went on sale. It went on sale twice in the six month period I was watching it and each time it was sold for a discount of $50 off the $400 asking price. The best price I was able to find online was $325 plus $40 shipping, which adds up to a total cost of $365.

I decided that $350 was the best price I was going to get unless the item went on clearance, which I thought was unlikely for a generator. I watched the ads at my local hardware store and found a coupon that offered 15 percent off any purchase over a hundred dollars. It was good for a couple weeks. It just so happened that the generator went on sale for $350 at the same time, so I was able to get an additional 15% off of the sale price. The final cost was just under $300 before taxes for a generator that normally costs $400. I saved a hundred dollars that can now be used for other survival gear.

You don't have to buy all of the items on your list new. Many items are just as good used as they are new and will cost you pennies on the dollar if you hunt them down in garage sales, flea markets and thrift stores.

I've seen $400 sleeping bags sold for $30 bucks at thrift stores near me. The bags were in good shape, too, and looked like they'd never been used. I've also seen tents, camp stove and generators for rock bottom prices, along with an assortment of tools and other supplies.

Don't forget to try to dicker down the price.

What I've found is you aren't going to have much luck at the big retailers like Wal-Mart or REI, but you may be able to talk your way into a better deal at privately-owned stores like surplus stores and stores catering to survivalists. Flea markets and garage sales are great places to practice wheeling and dealing, as most people expect to sell their stuff at a low price.

The poor prepper knows that paying full price will empty his or her pockets and leave them with little to show for it. Work on finding the best deals and your money will stretch a lot further than it otherwise would.

Stockpiling Food the Cheap and Easy Way

Sure, it would be nice to have a stockpile of MREs and freeze-dried foods you could pack up and take off with in an emergency. They're light weight and easy to move if you can't stay in your home.

They're also expensive. Stockpiling enough food to feed 4 adults (or two adults and two older children) two of these meals a day will cost you between $400 and $600 dollars depending on how fancy the meals you buy are. If you want to stock up a 6 month supply of food, you're looking at $2,500 or more in food costs alone.

And believe me when I tell you the food in these kits isn't anything to write home about. You'll get your best deals when you buy your food in bulk, but you aren't going to want to eat the same thing every day for the next 6 months. Especially when you're going to be tired of it after the first couple days.

You're going to want at least 2,000 calories worth of food each day per adult and around 1,500 per kid. While this is a good rule of thumb, it's important you realize not all calories are created equal. Calories obtained from eating a bag of chocolate candy aren't equal to calories from a bowl of vegetable soup. The soup will be more filling and will provide more nutrition. You aren't going to last long if you're consuming 2,000 calories worth of junk food a day.

You're going to want to steer clear of empty calories that don't add any nutritional value. Every food you put into storage should add something of value to your diet.

The good news is you can stockpile enough normal food to keep you supplied for at least 6 month without even using your prepping budget. This allows you to keep your prepping budget free for the other items on your list, like a campstove, propane canisters, a can opener and cooking and eating utensils.

Every time you go shopping for food, pick up an extra item or two that you can add to your emergency stockpile. You're going to want to keep your stockpile somewhere other than where you keep the rest of your food or you're going to be tempted to use the food you're stockpiling when you run out.

$10 here, $5 bucks there. A little at a time, you can gradually build up a respectable stockpile of food, all without busting your budget. In fact, if done correctly, you won't even notice the few extra bucks you're spending each week on your emergency food. Over time, you'll build up a decent stockpile of food you'll actually want to eat.

To further save money, watch for sales on canned goods and other non-perishable items to get them at rock-bottom prices. Most items in the store will go on sale once every couple of months. Save up coupons and take advantage of sales and you'll get even more food.

Take advantage of the deals available at your local dollar-store or dented cans store. These places sell the same canned goods that are sold in regular stores at a deep discount. The dented goods stores sell food that the regular stores can't sell because the cans are dented or the boxes are torn open a little. The canned goods are often sold for ½ the price they are in regular stores. I recently purchased a bunch of cans of Campbell's Soup that normally sell for around a buck each for $0.30 a can.

Be sure to keep an eye on the expiration dates on your food supply. As the foods in your emergency storage start to age, rotate them into your pantry and rotate newer foods into your emergency stores. An emergency supply of food intended to last 6 months isn't going to do you much good if everything expires the first month after an emergency. You'll probably still be able to eat most of it, but you'll have to be extra cautious to make sure your food is good. If you ask me, it's a worry you don't need, and one that's easy to avoid if you rotate your food regularly.

Not all foods are ideal for emergency storage. You need to avoid foods that won't last and foods with expiration dates that are approaching.

Here are some of the foods you can buy a few cans, boxes or packages at a time that will last long enough to make them worth adding to your emergency supplies:

- Bottled water. Buy it by the gallon to save money.
- Breakfast cereal. Be sure to rotate your cereal frequently to avoid it getting stale.
- Canned fruit.
- Canned meats.
- Canned soups.
- Canned vegetables.
- Cereal.
- Coffee.

- Condiments like ketchup, mustard, etc. There's no reason your food has to be eaten plain. This stuff can be purchased for a dollar a container and it lasts a long time.
- Dried beans.
- Dried fruit.
- Dry noodles and pasta.
- Flour.
- Granola and granola bars.
- Jam and jelly.
- Jerky.
- Noodle cups.
- Nuts.
- Packets of dry gravy, sauce, dressing.
- Peanut butter.
- Powdered milk.
- Protein bars
- Ready-made foods like Rice-a-Roni and macaroni and cheese.
- Rice.
- Salt and pepper.
- Sauces.
- Seeds.
- Spices.
- Top Ramen.
- Trail mix.

Try to build up a wide variety of foods. Sure, it would be nice if you could just buy a 6 month supply of Top

Ramen at $0.10 a pack, but you aren't going to want to try to live on just Top Ramen for that long.

You'll get tired of eating the same thing for every meal and your body won't get the nutrition it needs. It's OK to include some Top Ramen, but you're going to want other foods to break up the monotony.

Here's a tip that a lot of people don't think about when purchasing supplies.

Some of the foods you're probably going to want stockpile may be high in sodium. These high-sodium foods are going to make you thirsty and will up your body's need for water, which may not be ideal in an emergency because access to clean water may be limited. Avoiding high sodium foods will help you keep your water needs to a minimum.

Here's another tip that can save you cash.

Instead of buying condiments, grab a few extra packets of ketchup, mayo, mustard and taco sauce whenever you go to a fast food restaurant. These packets will stay good for up to 6 months, so be sure to rotate your stock.

Preserving Your Own Foods at Home

There are a number of safe methods you can use to preserve your favorite foods at home. Canning and drying and the two most common methods you can use to save foods for an emergency situation.

I've also seen people recommend freezing foods, but this isn't an ideal method because if you lose power, you could potentially lose a lot of food when it melts and starts to spoil. The other methods of preservation don't require electricity to keep the food fresh and are much better options.

Food preservation methods allow you to take advantage of sales on fruit, vegetables and meats. When you find a good deal, buy extra and then preserve it for later use. You'll be able to build up a good stock of canned and dried foods in no time. Be sure to rotate your stock every six months to a year. You don't want to go to your emergency food supply only to find everything has spoiled because it's been in there for years.

Canning

Canning involves placing food in a jar and heating it to a temperature that kills off bacteria and other harmful microorganisms. This heating and subsequent cooling seals the jars, making them airtight. This prevents bacteria from getting in and causing the food to spoil.

There are two safe methods of canning.

The water bath canning method is the easiest method and can be used to safely can acidic foods like fruits and tomatoes. With water bath canning, you fill a large pot with water, heat it up and use the hot water to kill off any microorganisms in the jar while sealing the jar shut.

A pressure canner is required for canning meats, vegetables and other foods that have low acid content. Pressure canners up the temperature to 240 degrees F, which will kill off botulism and other microorganisms found in low-acid foods. These microorganisms can survive the water bath canning method, so don't use it for low acid foods.

The following methods of canning are considered unsafe and shouldn't be used:

- **Inversion canning.** This method involves adding hot food to a jar and turning the jar upside down to get it to seal. This method doesn't kill off any airborne bacteria that may have landed on the jar or the food while it was being transferred.
- **Steam canning.** Uses steam, but no pressure. Doesn't adequately heat up the jars of food and some bacteria may survive.
- **Solar canning.** Uses the sun to heat up the food, but fails to get food hot enough to kill all bacteria.
- **Microwave canning.** Using the microwave doesn't evenly heat the food. You might also cause the jars you're using to explode.

There are a number of other methods of canning in use, many of which date back hundreds of years. Pressure canning and water bath canning are the only two methods that are considered safe. Using any other method may allow harmful microorganisms to survive the process.

Drying Food

Dehydration, or drying, is another popular method of preserving foods so they can be stored for long periods of time. It allows you to save extra fruit, vegetables and meat, so you can eat them months down the road. Dried foods have a lot of the moisture removed from them, which creates an environment in which microorganisms aren't able to thrive.

There are a number of methods used to dry foods.

Some of the more common methods include using an oven, the sun or a commercial dehydrator. You need to maintain a constant temperature of 135 to 140 degrees F while circulating air past the food in order to remove the moisture that evaporates away. Failure to maintain a constant temperature or keep air circulating can cause your food to develop a dry crust before the inside dries out or it may start to spoil before it's dry.

You can dry fruit, meat, fish and even some vegetables. Place them in airtight containers after drying and check them for signs of moisture after a week. If there's condensation in the container, the food needs more drying. Return it to the dryer. Once your food is dry, store it in an airtight container in a cool, dark location. Most dried foods will last from 6 months to a year if properly dried and stored.

Don't Forget the Vitamins

Canned, freeze-dried and powdered foods are sorely lacking in the vitamins and minerals your body needs to survive. They'll hold you over in the event of a short emergency, but aren't nutritious enough for long-term use.

You're going to want to keep vitamin and mineral supplements on hand to make sure your body is getting everything it needs. Having the nutrients your body needs will ensure you're able to think clearly and will boost your immune system so it's able to fight off illness and disease.

The following vitamins and minerals should be in your stockpile:

- **Multivitamins.** Multivitamins contain a number of vitamins and minerals the human body needs to function correctly. I recommend keeping a year's supply of multivitamins for each member of your family. Make sure you choose the right type of multivitamin for each member of your family. There are men's, women's, children's vitamins and there are multivitamins suited specifically for the elderly.
- **Vitamin A.** Vitamin A helps with healthy bones, gums and teeth.
- **B Vitamins.** These vitamins aid with healthy cell formation and they help the body break down and process nutrients.
- **Vitamin C.** Boosts your immune and nervous system.

- **Probiotics and enzymes.** Aid with food digestion and keep your digestive system functioning properly.

Keeping the right vitamins in your emergency supplies can help make sure your family stays healthy during an extended crisis event. Without the proper nutrition, you become more susceptible to illness and disease and won't be able to think clearly.

Creating a Sustainable Food Supply

There may come a time when 6 months of food isn't enough.

In a major emergency that renders the government unable to rebuild for a long period of time, you're going to need a sustainable food supply. What this means is you're going to have to be able to grow and/or raise your own food. You're also going to want to have the skills and supplies on hand to be able to both hunt and fish for additional food.

Seed Saving

Starting a garden, no matter how small, will provide you with food for your table. It will also provide you a source of seeds you can use to grow new crops year-in and year-out. You'll be able to grow a crop, harvest the seeds and then use the seeds you've harvested to grow another crop.

Just because you have a garden doesn't mean it's sustainable. The only way your garden is going to work is if you're able to harvest seeds from it to replant the following season. If you're ordering hybrid seeds from a manufacturer and your supply of hybrid seeds dries up, you aren't going to be able to continue growing food. You'll be high and dry as soon as the seeds you have on hand run out. While you can save hybrid seeds and plant them the following season, you aren't going to get the same quality of vegetables you grew the previous season. In fact, you could get something that's barely edible.

The only way to go when you're trying to grow a sustainable garden is to use pure or heirloom seeds. Plants grown from these seeds will produce seeds that grow into plants just like their parents. Save seeds from the biggest and strongest plants in your crop and soon you'll have your own super-breed of plant tailored to suit your needs and local growing conditions.

If you're interested in saving seeds, your best bet is to plant a garden and get started now. There's a bit of a learning curve involved, and it's best you make your mistakes while there are seeds available you can use to restart your garden. Once you get the hang of seed saving, it's pretty easy, and you'll soon have a collection of seeds you can use to grow your own food wherever you go.

Seeds last anywhere from 3 to 5 years, so be sure to rotate your seed stock. You can't just throw a few containers of seeds in your emergency kit and forget about them. When it comes time to sprout and plant them, you may end up sorely disappointed . . . and starving.

Animals You Can Raise for Food

Animals are another sustainable food source.

Unless you live in the country, your neighbors probably aren't going to appreciate you turning your backyard into a farm. What this means is cows, pigs and other large livestock is probably out of the question. While most people don't have the space (or the desire, for that matter) to raise large animals for food, you can easily raise small animals like rabbits and chickens in most areas.

When it comes to chickens, you're going to need a place to put your coop. Chickens can be a bit noisy, so you're going to need to keep your coop as far away from your neighbors as possible. When it comes to sustainability, you're going to need at least one rooster with your flock to fertilize the eggs your hens are laying. Without a rooster present, hens will lay eggs, but they won't be able to be hatched into chicks. What this means is you'll get plenty of eggs until your hens grow old, but you'll never get any chicks. Once your hens die off, you won't have chickens or eggs any more.

Adding a rooster or two into the mix allows you to hatch and raise new chicks. When you hatch chicks, they're generally be a 50-50 mix of hens and roosters, you can raise the hens to maturity as egg-laying hens and eat the roosters when they reach 3 to 6 months of age. This will keep you in constant supply of both eggs and chicken meat.

The problem with roosters is they tend to get noisy early in the morning. This propensity to crow in the morning (and any time during the day they feel the need) has led many cities to allow laying hens, but outlaw roosters altogether. I happen to live in one such city, and I've found a way around it—well, sort of. One thing's for certain, there's no way you can hide a mature rooster. It's going to sound off early in the morning and tick everyone in your neighborhood off.

What you can hide are rooster chicks.

Roosters don't start crowing right away. Some start crowing within a month. Others can take 6 months or longer to start crowing. I've even owned a couple that never crowed. If you're lucky enough to stumble across one of the quiet roosters, you'll be able to sustain your chicken population no matter what the rules state. Most cities aren't going to check your flock for roosters unless someone complains about the noise. No noise equals no complaints.

Keep your rooster chicks until they start crowing, then either give them away or butcher them for their meat. You should seek to always have at least a few rooster chicks on hand. That way, if there is a major interruption to the food supply, you can let your chicks grow into roosters that will be capable of growing your flock.

The main reason people keep chickens around is because they want a sustainable source of eggs. You can reasonably expect 3 eggs per day for every 5 hens you have that are of laying age.

Keep in mind that this is under optimal conditions and your hens may or may not lay at this pace. Egg production can be affected by a number of factors, including stress, daylight and cold weather. Make sure you have breeds of chicken that thrive in the climate in which you plan on raising them to maximize egg production.

Rabbits are another good animal to raise for food. As long as you have room for a hutch, you can raise rabbits. I know a guy who has a hutch on the balcony of his apartment and he's been raising rabbits for years. It isn't ideal, but he believes in keeping a sustainable source of food around just in case.

Rabbits are prolific breeders and they will reproduce quickly. If you need meat, rabbits are a good source that will replenish quickly.

Fish

While most people don't have enough property to build a pond they can stock with fish, you can keep a fishing pole and some light tackle on hand. This will allow you to catch fish from lakes, rivers, ponds and even the ocean, if it's close-by. You can keep some fishing lures on hand, or you can catch your own worms for bait by luring them out of the ground.

There are two ways I've used to lure worms from the ground that work well.

One's a little safer than the other. The safer method is to hammer a metal pipe into a wet patch of ground and leave about 6 inches exposed. Use a metal hammer to tap on the side of the pipe. The vibrations will cause worms to rise up out of the ground. You might have to continuously tap the pipe for as long as a half hour to call the worms up. I don't know why this method works; it just does. I've had mixed results using this method. Sometimes it works great and other times it doesn't seem to work at all.

The other method is to use electricity.

I'm not going to include a tutorial here because there is the very real possibility of you getting electrocuted and I don't want to be sued, but the gist of it is to hook wires up to a large nail, drive the nail into the ground and then connect the wires to the positive and negative terminals on a small battery. And no, a car battery doesn't qualify as a small battery. My dad used to use this method when we went to visit my grandmother and the worms would come dancing out of the ground like they were swaying back and forth to a beat only they could hear.

Fishing is somewhat of a lost art these days. Those who have never been fishing and don't know how probably won't be able to catch enough fish to feed their family in an emergency. If you've been fishing and understand how to fish, then you may be able to catch dinner time and time again, especially if you fish places that were previously off-limits to the general public.

Here are some good places to try:

- Drainage areas that have a constant supply of water.
- Farm ponds.
- Irrigation ponds and canals.
- Ponds on private property. Just don't get shot by the owner!
- Golf course and cemetery ponds.
- Small streams where fishing was previously banned.
- Drinking water reservoirs.
- Rock quarries.

If you've fished local lakes and reservoirs, you probably have a good idea of where to go and catch fish. If you've never had any luck at the local places, try the places on the list above. They're usually full of fish that are more than willing to bite because they haven't seen the pressure the other places have.

Catfish are a hardy breed of fish you can raise almost anywhere. A catfish can live in a muddy hole in the ground. I didn't believe this until my brother tossed one he didn't feel like cleaning into his backyard on a rainy day. It flopped around until it came to rest in a puddle that was a couple feet deep and stayed there until the rain stopped and the puddle dried up.

I've heard stories of people raising catfish in barrels. They put them in there as fingerlings and toss in their leftover food for the catfish to eat. Months down the road, they dump out the barrel and harvest the catfish.

Other Animals You Can Eat (If You Have to)

I'm going to warn you in advance that this section is probably going to gross you out a bit. It may also help you survive if you find yourself in a situation where you're in need of a sustainable food source.

The following animals can be raised and eaten if you need food:

- **Pigeons.** These birds can be raised and bred in the city and they aren't as noisy as chickens. Some people like the taste of pigeon and some don't care for it. I say if you're hungry enough, you'll eat anything.
- **Bees.** You're going to need a bit of space if you're going to keep bees. If you have the room, bees can be used as a source of both beeswax and honey.
- **Rodents.** The thought of eating a rat or a guinea pig grosses most people out. They're edible; they breed prolifically and will populate the Earth long after the last person is dead and gone.

- **Goats.** Goats can be raised in a relatively small area and they'll eat anything you give them. They will provide you with both meat and milk. If you're wondering what goat meat tastes like, check your local grocery store. I've seen it for sale in mine from time to time.
- **Pigs.** You can raise a pig or two in a relatively small pen. Pigs will eat anything. You can feed them your leftover food scraps and they'll be happy. Hogs reach a couple hundred pounds in less than a year and can be harvested for a lot of meat when the need arises.
- **Quail.** These small birds are small enough to be raised in cages or a coop. They're good to eat and you can even eat their tiny eggs if you're looking for a quick and tasty snack.

Water, Water, Everywhere

In an emergency situation, you may find yourself surrounded by water and still not have anything to drink. Drinking contaminated water can make you sick and you'll end up dehydrated and needing water even more. One thing's for certain. Without drinkable water, you're probably going to die in less than a week. Most people will last 3 to 5 days without water. Any more than that and you're at serious risk.

You're going to be miserable after one day without water. After two, it'll be all you can think about. Three days and you're going to be on death's door. You don't want to get stuck without water. If I had to choose between storing only food or only water, I'd store as much water as humanly possible. The biggest mistake you can make is to assume you're going to be able to find clean water.

You're going to want at least 4 quarts of water to drink per person per day. This equates to roughly 182.5 gallons of water per person over a 6-month period of time. A family of 4 will require 730 gallons of water over 6 months' time. You're probably staring at the screen right now with your mouth open. If you're anything like the average person, you've probably got a few packs of bottled water put away and not much more. This will last you a few days in the event of an emergency. You're going to need a lot more.

Let me try to put this in perspective.

Let's say for the sake of argument that the average bottle of water contains 16.9 ounces of water. I know at least one major brand does because I've got a bottle sitting here in front of me. This equates to roughly 0.5 quarts of water per bottle. A single person is going to need 1,460 of these water bottles over a 6-month period of time. A family of four is going to need 5,840 bottles of water. If there are 24 bottles to a pack, you're going to need 61 packages of bottled water just to meet a single person's need. That's roughly 244 packages of water for a family of four. At $3 a pack, you're looking at more than $700 just to buy the water—and then you've got to find somewhere to store it.

You can buy five-gallon water bottles that you fill yourself for around $10 bucks each if you find them on sale. The problem lies in the fact that you're going to need 182.5 of these bottles per person. Again, storage space and the $1820.50 per person cost make this infeasible.

50 gallon water barrels are another option, but are really only feasible if you have a garage or storage shed to keep them in. You're going to want at least 3 of these full of water per person in your house. They cost around $100 a barrel, so you're going to end up paying around $300 per person. The nice thing about these is you can outfit them with kits that allow you to hook up to your rain gutters and catch rain water to refill the barrels.

The reality is most people aren't going to store enough water to last 6 months. Most aren't even going to have enough to last 3 months.

What I suggest doing is storing as much water as you can afford and have space for. You can buy it a couple packs at a time when you find it on sale or you can buy one five gallon container a month and stack them in a closet or your basement. I prefer the smaller water bottles because they're easier to stack and store. I keep a few 5-gallon containers full in case I have to pack up in a hurry and hit the road and I've got a couple 50-gallon barrels in my storage shed that I can use if I'm able to stay at home.

Store your water in a cool, dark area and rotate your stock. I try to switch all of my water bottles out every 6 months and I refill my 5- and 50- gallon containers once every 4 months.

What to Do If You're Caught without Water

Sometimes an emergency catches us off-guard. You may find yourself low on water from the get-go, or you may be on the verge of using up the water you had stored. Either way, you're going to need water, and fast.

If you know there's an emergency on the horizon or an emergency has taken place, but your water still works (and is safe) for the time being, it's time to get to work. You need to fill every container in the house with water. Buckets, bags, glasses, dishes, bowls, etc. Fill them all. You can even create make-shift bag from a plastic tarp and twine to hold large amounts of water.

Here are some ideas of items you can store water in:

- Bowls.
- Buckets.
- Cups.
- Dishes.
- Empty cans and bottles.
- Pans.
- Plastic bags.
- Plastic storage bins.
- Pots.
- Sinks.
- Tarps.
- Your bathtub. Buy a WaterBOB or two, which is a bag that fits into your tub and allows you to bag up a tub's worth of water. A couple of these

bags will allow you to store a couple hundred gallons of water.

The idea is to save as much water as you can while you still know it's potable. If you aren't sure, you're going to have to disinfect it. We'll get to that later on in this chapter.

If you know the water supply has been contaminated, turn off the water supply to your house. This will prevent contaminated water from getting in. You won't have much by way of running water, but you may be able to get clean water from the following places:

- Faucets.
- Hot water tank.
- Ice in the fridge. Get it before it melts because some iceboxes aren't waterproof.
- Pipes.
- Toilet tank.
- Your toilet bowl. Don't drink this water unless you disinfect it first.

Can You Safely Drink Pool Water?

Another source of water you wouldn't think of unless you have one is a swimming pool or hot tub. If you don't have one, I'll bet one of your neighbors does. An in-ground pool can hold more than 20,000 gallons of water. An above-ground pool usually holds between 5,000 and 10,000. A pool at a local rec center or high school may have as much as 50,000 gallons of water in it.

This water is only going to be good for the first week or two after an accident, and only then if it hasn't been contaminated. Granted the owners took proper care of their pool and you get to it soon enough, the water in the pool may be potable without needing treatment.

When it comes to survival, the chlorine content of a pool is both a bane and a boon. The chlorine is what keeps the water safe from bacteria and algae growth. This is good, to a certain point. Water with 4 parts per million of chlorine or less is considered safe to consume. Most swimming pools have between 1 and 4 ppm of chlorine, which makes the water safe for consumption. That is, unless they've recently been shock treated, which can bump the levels of chlorine up to as high as 30 ppm.

If you own the pool, you'll know whether or not you've recently done a shock treatment and you'll have a pretty good idea of whether or not your water is safe. If you have to harvest water from someone else's pool, it's a good idea to test it to see what the chlorine level is before consuming the water. Chlorine test strips are inexpensive, so it's a good idea to keep some on hand in your emergency supply kit.

When left uncovered, the chlorine in a pool begins to break down and the pool will begin to develop algae in less than a week. Never drink water from a pool that has visible algae growth without first treating the water. You also want to avoid drinking untreated water from a pool that may have been contaminated with flood water.

Making Possibly Contaminated Water Safer to Drink

Aside from swimming pools, there are a number of other places outside the home you can get water from. Here are a few places to try:

- Lakes.
- Rivers.
- Ponds.
- Streams.
- Irrigation canals.
- Rainwater.
- Water storage containers.
- Natural springs.

The problem with using these sources of water is they could be contaminated. You won't be able to tell by looking at the water or smelling it. The bacteria and contaminants lurking beneath the surface aren't always visible to the naked eye and can make you deathly ill. Toxic chemicals, bacteria, disease and heavy metals are just a handful of the contaminants you need to be worried about.

Avoid drinking outside water at all costs. You shouldn't use any of these water sources unless you absolutely have to. That said, the situation may arise where you either obtain water from an outside source and use it . . . or die.

When you have to use potentially contaminated water sources, there are a handful of things you can do to the water to make it safer. There's no guarantee it'll be completely safe, but taking the following steps will at least make it safer:

1. Filter it.

Coffee filters are an inexpensive way to filter out large pieces of sediment and other large particles from your water. You're going to want some coffee filters in your emergency supplies. If you don't have any coffee filters (or you run out), you can strain your water through a cloth T-shirt.

Another method of filtration is to trickle your water through sand. Collect a bucket of sand and slowly drip the water through the sand. A lot of the sediment will get filtered out on the way through.

The best method of filtration is to use charcoal. You can keep a few charcoal filters on hand in case you need them. If you don't have any filters around, you can make your own. Light a wood fire and let it burn out. Let the charcoals cool and collect them in container. Filter the water through the charcoal. As the water passes the charcoal, the carbon in the charcoal will combine with most toxins and keep them in the filter.

2. Boil it.

After you've filtered the water to get rid of toxins, you're going to want to boil it. Boiling water kills off most of the bacteria and living organisms in the water. Combining steps 1 and 2 make your water safer than just boiling it or just filtering it.

Bring your water to a rolling boil for at least 5 minutes.

3. Treat it.

According to the Center for Disease Control (CDC), you can chlorinate your water with household bleach that contains 5.25 to 6 percent sodium hypochlorite as its sole active ingredient. Add 8 to 10 drops of bleach per gallon of water, stir it and let it sit for a half hour. A teaspoon of bleach can be used to disinfect 5 gallons of water.

If the water doesn't have a slight chlorine smell after treating it, you shouldn't drink it. Chlorinating your water is a safe and easy way of killing off bacteria and viruses.

You can also use hydrogen peroxide to clean your water, but it isn't as effective as chlorinating it.

Distillation

By filtering, boiling and treating your water, you'll get rid of a lot of contaminants. There's no guarantee you'll get rid of everything and you could still end up drinking water with some contaminants in it. The goal is to make your water as safe as possible.

Another method you can use to even further clean your water is distillation, which will remove even more contaminants. To distill your water, you need to heat it up until it becomes steam and then condense the steam back into water. One method that can be used to do this involves placing a smaller container of water inside a larger container. Place a lid on the larger container and heat it up. The water inside the smaller container will begin to boil and will condense on the lid of the larger container.

The water that condenses on the lid will be clean water that's free of almost all contamination. It may take some time to collect enough water to drink this way, but at least you'll know it's relatively safe.

Let There Be Light

Your preparedness kit should have at least 4 sources of light, a couple of which don't require electricity. You're going to need light to see in the dark when the power is out and your family will feel much safer when you have the ability to check on anything that goes bump in the night.

Having adequate light is especially important when you have young children because they'll feel much better if they're able to see at night. Young kids tend to be scared of the dark, and you don't want to have to deal with a scared child on top of the rest of the stress you're already under.

Candles

Candles have come a long way in recent years.

The old-school wax candles that drip wax as you burn them are still around and can be purchased on the cheap. These candles can be purchased for around $0.30 each if you buy them in bulk and will last about an hour for each inch they are long.

Go with a bigger candle with a larger diameter and you'll get more burn time. A 2-inch diameter candle will last you 8 to 10 hours per inch, while a 4-inch candle will burn for as long as 30 to 40 hours for each inch of height. These larger candles will cost more than the tapered wax candles of old, but they more than make up for it in burn time.

You can also find emergency candles designed to last as long as long as 120 hours. Paraffin candles are good emergency candles, but they can be a bit on the expensive side. Liquid paraffin candles can be purchased for around $7 each and will last for 100 hours or more.

Glow Sticks

Glow sticks can be a quick and easy source of light when you need it fast. All you have to do is bend the glow stick until the tube containing the hydrogen peroxide breaks open and then shake it up.

You'll have an instant light source that lasts up to 12 hours.

Here's a tip most people don't know. Heating your glow stick up will make it brighter. Place your glow stick in hot water for up to a minute to get it to emit a much brighter light.

Flashlights

Flashlights are the number one light source people have in their home.

You're going to want to add at least 3 flashlights to your emergency kit. Don't count the flashlights you have laying around the house in drawers or in the garage. Those are extras. You need to have three new flashlights that you've tested to make sure they work and then removed the batteries and placed them with your emergency supplies. It also doesn't hurt to have flashlights near each bed in the house, so family members can find their way around in the event of a power outage.

The good news is you can get decent flashlights for cheap. I recommend buying a couple LED flashlights that advertise thousands of hours of light with minimal battery consumption. The LED lights are long-lasting and tougher to break than conventional flashlights. You should also have one of the larger Mag lights in your kit. An LED headlight is also a good idea, so you can work in the dark without having to hold a flashlight.

As far as batteries go, I see a lot of people recommending rechargeable batteries. These are great as long as you have a way to recharge them. There are solar battery recharging systems on the market that harness the power of the sun. GoalZero offers a nice kit for around $100 once you factor in the required accessories.

I personally don't recommend relying solely on rechargeable batteries. They're nice to have, but never seem to last as long as regular name-brand batteries. Stock up on regular batteries and keep the rechargeable batteries as back-up. Whenever you find the batteries your flashlight uses on sale, buy an extra pack or two and put them away. Before long, you'll have more than enough batteries to last through all but the longest of emergencies.

Don't forget extra bulbs. Again, buy a pack of bulbs here and there when you can afford them and soon you'll have a good supply built up.

Lanterns

No, I'm not talking about the cheap imitation Coleman lanterns that run on batteries. I'm talking the good kind that uses mantles and propane. Keep a real lantern on hand and you'll be able to light up an entire area at night, no matter how much wind there is.

Just don't keep your lantern lit in an unventilated area. They use oxygen up as they burn and carbon monoxide can build up and cause injury or even death.

Oil Lamps

Oil lamps are somewhat of a relic from the days of old. They consist of a glass enclosure that houses a wick that extends into a reservoir full of lamp oil. The oil seeps up the wick and when you light it, the oil in the lamp creates a flame that provides light. A full reservoir of oil will last between 15 and 20 hours. When the oil runs out, you can refill the reservoir and keep using the light.

Oil lights are cheap. An inexpensive one will run you $15. You should also buy extra wicks and a bunch of lamp oil to refill the lamp when it runs out.

Don't Forget the Fun

Try to spend an entire day without electricity and you'll be struck by just how reliant we've become on items that run on electricity. While most preppers seek to build up a cache of supplies that replace the electric items we've all become reliant on, there's one area where most prepper's stockpiles fall well short of the mark.

You wouldn't normally associate an emergency situation with entertainment, but let's imagine a situation in which you have to hunker down for months on end without electricity. You aren't in imminent danger and don't have to spend your days on high alert and you find yourself sitting around for long periods of time with nothing to do. While the adults in your family may be able to handle this sort of boredom without too much fanfare, the kids in the family are going to be bored to death.

No phones, no television, no computers, no Internet, no Facebook, no video games. The list goes on and on. For many of today's kids, no electricity equals no fun whatsoever.

You're going to want to keep some items in your stockpile to help fight off boredom. This is especially important if you have kids. Keep an eye out for good deals on the following items and pick them up when they go on sale:

- Board games.
- Cards.
- Card games like Uno and Go Fish.

- Books.
- Magazines.
- Puzzles.
- Crossword puzzle books.
- Word game books.
- Arts and crafts materials.
- Coloring books.

Keep whatever you buy out of the hands of your children until an emergency, so the stuff is new to them when you break it out. This stuff may help ease some of the boredom associated with being forced off the grid.

Bugging Out vs. Bugging In

Whenever possible, you should stay in the comfort of your own home. This is called bugging in or hunkering down. Even if the power's out and you don't have running water, your home is going to be your safest bet when it comes to survival. As long as there isn't an imminent threat that forces you from your home, there's no good reason to leave the safety and comfort of your own home unless you absolutely have to.

There are a number of reasons you should stay home. First and foremost, you have much better shelter from the elements at home. You also have access to your entire cache of survival gear and all of the food you have stockpiled. Another good reason is you're familiar with your home and the surrounding area and will be more comfortable if you have to defend it.

Your other option is bugging out, which entails grabbing what you can and heading for a safer location.

If you're lucky, you'll have time to grab as much gear and food as possible before you head out. If not, you'd better have a bug out bag packed and ready to go. We'll cover the bug out bag in the next chapter. Basically, it's a bag that contains everything you need to survive for at least 72 hours. When a threat forces you from your home, you grab the bag on your way out the door and head for your bug out location.

When people think of bugging out, they more often than not think of heading out into the wilderness to a safe location, distant from other human beings. This is rarely the best choice. In most situations, you'd be much better of bugging out to another city, county or state while staying on the grid. You can reach an agreement with a distant friend or relative where you can head to their place in the event there's an emergency that forces you from your home in return for them being able to do the same if the need arises.

There are very few situations in which bugging out is better than bugging in and even fewer where bugging out into the wilderness is your best option. If you can stay home and stick things out, you should, unless there's a threat looming, like an enemy invasion, a flood or a fire headed your way. When you do make the decision to bug out, look at all of your options and choose the best one.

If there's a flood or a fire headed your way, it doesn't make any sense to head into the hills. You'll be much better off getting out of the way of the threat and waiting it out while remaining a part of society. On the other hand, if zombies are running rampant and leaving entire cities in shambles, your best bet is going to be bugging out to a remote location where very few, if any, zombies are going to stumble across your path.

You need to assess the situation and choose the option that gives you the best chance of survival.

Keep your options open and weigh the potential risk vs. reward of each of your options. Don't let emotions control your decisions. Instead, take a deep breath and let logic be your guide. You don't want to bug out every time you think there's a threat because you'll quickly run out of money and supplies. You need to assess each threat and determine how likely it is to come to fruition. If you live in earthquake country and bug out every time the ground trembles, you're going to constantly be on the run. On the other hand, if a 7.0 strikes, followed by a number of violent aftershocks, it would be a good idea to get out of dodge until things settle down a bit.

Don't put off making the decision to leave until it's too late. You don't want to leave unless you have to, but sticking around too long can be every bit as dangerous.

A large number of people did this during Hurricane Katrina and ended up trapped by the floodwaters, unable to get away. These were the people you saw sitting on top of their roofs in the hot sun, baking as they waited for rescue. These are also the people you saw being carted away in body bags. More than 4,000 people died as a result of Katrina, most of which would still be alive today if they would have heeded government warnings and left when they were told to.

Bug in whenever possible, but prepare yourself to bug out if need be. If you're able to hunker down and stay in place, you'll still be able to use the gear in your bug out bag for survival. You'll be prepared no matter what.

The Bug Out Bag: Why You Need One and What You Need to Have In It

If you're new to the world of prepping, you may not have heard of BOB. He's your best friend in the event you have to leave the comfort of your home and strike off to a distant location. BOB will help you make it to your destination alive and intact. BOB is, of course, your Bug Out Bag.

A bug out bag is a bag packed full of everything you need to survive for at least 72 hours outside of your home. Once you've been prepping for a while, you can build your bag up so it has enough in it to last you for a much longer time, but 72 hours is a good amount of time to shoot for initially.

When an emergency situation forces you out of your home, all you have to do is grab your bug out bag—or bags, if you have a family—and head for the hill, or wherever it is you're planning on bugging out to. Having a bag at the ready allows you to grab a single bag that contains everything you need to survive for days on your own in one fell swoop. This will allow you to save precious time and possibly get out of town ahead of the masses, beating any traffic jams or other roadblocks that may arise.

It's a good idea to have a bag packed for each member of your family that is capable of carrying one. That includes smaller bags for young children and a bag for the family dog.

What you put in your bug out bag is going to depend on your personal needs and the location you plan on bugging out to. The rest of the chapter should help you determine what you need in your bag.

The Bag

The bag you choose to carry your supplies in is probably going to be the most important choice you make. You're going to want a bag that's durable, yet light enough that it isn't too heavy. You don't know what sort of terrain you may end up carrying your bag through, so it's going to have to be tough enough to handle pretty much anything.

Make sure you get a big enough bag to carry the stuff you need it to carry. I like the bags that have MOLLE-compatible webbing, because they allow you to attach even more gear to the outside of the bag.

I wish I could tell you there was a cheap way out when it comes to buying the bag, but there really isn't. You're going to have to spend at least a hundred bucks to get a good quality bag that's built to last. It helps to remember that it doesn't matter how much gear you have if your bag falls apart and you aren't able to carry it.

You can get good 72-hour bags from the following places. I'm not affiliated with them and get nothing if you go to these sites and buy a bag. I'm simply trying to make your job easier.

5.11 Tactical

http://www.511tactical.com/All-Products/Bags-Backpacks/Backpacks.html

5.11 Tactical carries good bags that range from $100 to $300. Keep a close eye on their site, as they often offer sales that give customers 10 to 20 percent off of everything on the site. They also offer free shipping for purchases over $100.

Maxpedition

http://www.maxpedition.com/store/pc/Backpacks-c12.htm

Maxpedition offers good bags for between $100 and $200. I've found that you can often find the bags for sale on Amazon for less than what they cost direct from Maxpedition. The Vulture II is the best bag they offer. It's currently priced at around $175 bucks on Maxpedition's site, but you can find it for around $140 on Amazon.

Sandpiper

http://shop.sandpiperca.com/index.php/gear-packs.html

Sandpiper of California offers a number of good bug out bags. They also sell rolling load-out bags, which can be loaded up with a bunch of gear and loaded into a car or truck. Just make sure the vehicle you plan on using can accommodate the bag. Most Sandpiper bags cost between $100 and $200. They offer a couple sub-$100 bags that are of pretty good quality if you can't afford one of the more expensive bags.

The Contents of the Bag

You're going to have to put some thought into the contents of your bag. You're going to want to be able to survive for 72 hours at a bare minimum. You might have to survive for a much longer period of time. The more you pack with that in mind, the better off you'll be if you have to spend a significant amount of time on the run or at a remote location.

The contents of your bag will largely determine whether or not you'll make it to your destination intact and unharmed. Pack the wrong stuff and you could die. If not, you may end up extremely uncomfortable. Pack the right stuff and you'll be much better off. Survival isn't easy no matter how you look at it, but it can be made a lot easier if you have the right supplies.

Clothes

You're going to want to pack at least a change of clothes, maybe 2 changes depending on where you're headed and what the weather might be like. You need to pack whatever clothes you're going to need to make it through three days.

I know there are going to be some of my readers who read this and immediately think they don't need any extra clothes if they're only packing for three days. While you may not need extra clothes under optimal conditions, you're going to be sweaty, dirty and may have to cross rough or muddy terrain. Being able to change into a clean set of clothes before you bed down for the night could mean the difference between a good night's sleep and an uncomfortable night in the cold. You're also going to want to be able to change clothes if you rip holes in the clothes you're wearing.

You're going to want the following articles of clothing, at a bare minimum:

- Sweatshirt (or a coat, if it gets cold where you're headed).
- Poncho.
- Hiking boots.
- Pants.
- A hat.
- Long johns.
- A couple pairs of wicking socks.
- A couple shirts.

If you have room, you can pack more than this, but this is the least amount of clothing you should have.

If you're looking at cold winter weather, you're going to need more layers of warm clothing and a good winter coat capable of blocking out wind, rain, sleet and snow. You're also going to need extra changes of clothes because you're going to be miserable walking around wet all day. A good set of rain gear isn't cheap, but it can make a huge difference in inclement weather.

In the summer, you can pack lighter, but make sure you know what the weather is like where you're headed. Freak storms can hit in the middle of summer in the mountains that can dump an inch or two of rain in no time at all. If you get caught in one of these storms without the right gear for it, you're going to be miserable.

What I recommend in changing out your gear twice a year.

At the beginning of summer swap over to your summer clothing gear and lighten your pack. Take your winter gear and let it air out in a closet. If it's starting to smell musty, wash it and put it away for the summer. When fall rolls around and the nights start getting crisp, it's time to swap your winter gear back into your bug out bag. Take the summer stuff out and wash it and put it away. Your winter stuff is going to be bulkier and will take more room in your bag. If your bag is stuffed when your summer gear is in it, you're going to have to remove stuff to fit your winter gear in.

Choose wisely and don't take anything critical out of the bag.

Firearms and Ammo

When an emergency situation takes place that requires bugging out, there are going to be a lot of people caught unprepared. These people may see you leaving town with your gear and decide they want what you have. If you don't have guns, you may end up losing all of your gear to someone who does.

You're going to need firearms and ammo in order to protect yourself. Handguns are a good choice when you're travelling through the city because they're easily concealed and nobody will know you're armed until you let them know. Rifle and shotguns can be good deterrents if they're legal to carry in your area. People will see them and instantly know you're armed. This will deter most would-be thieves. They want an easy victim, not a firefight.

Guns aren't cheap, but you're going to want at least one dependable firearm and a few boxes of ammo. Keep your gun in your BOB and keep a loaded clip or two (or three) where they will be easy to access.

Make sure you know your local laws regarding carrying firearms and ammo. In a minor bug out situation in which you have to get out of town, you may not want to carry a loaded firearm in your bag. On the other hand, if your life is in danger and you're going to have to protect yourself and your family, you may not care about local law.

First Aid

Don't just buy a first aid kit and assume it has everything you're going to need. There's a very real possibility that your kit won't have the very items you need the most. There's also the possibility you won't know how to properly use the items in the kit even if it does have them.

Building your own kit will allow you to familiarize yourself with the contents of the kit and will go a long way toward ensuring you have everything you need. Again, take advantage of sales and closeout deals to get the items you need for pennies on the dollar.

Your first aid kit should (at the very least) contain these items:

- **Ace bandage.**
- **Aloe Vera gel.** Can be used to soothe burns, bug bites and all sorts of skin irritations.

- **Coagulants.** These can be used to stop heavy bleeding. Be aware that you can't leave the anticoagulant material in the wound forever. It's designed to help stop bleeding until you can get a person to the hospital to get the surgery they need. Do not use these unless you absolutely have to and keep them away from chest and abdominal wounds.
- **Antiseptic.**
- **Butterfly closure strips.** These can be used to close bigger wounds than you normally would be able to with regular bandages.
- **Cold pack.** You're going to want a few of these, as they're only good for one use.
- **Combat Application Tourniquet (CAT).** This handy tourniquet can be used to stop bleeding from the extremities. Make sure you're well-versed on the proper application of the tourniquet before an emergency situation arises. You don't want to try to learn how to use this item while you or someone else in your party is in danger of bleeding out.
- **Epinephrine autoinjector.** This handy tool can be used to treat anaphylactic shock, which is an intense allergic reaction. Those who swell up when they're stung by bees are suffering anaphylactic shock.
- **First aid handbook.** Even the most worthy of survivalists doesn't know how to handle every situation that requires first aid assistance. You're going to know even less. Keep a first aid

handbook in your bag and you'll up your chances of being able to handle basic and possibly even advanced first aid situations.

- **Gauze.** Get the biggest gauze you can. You can cut it down to smaller sizes if the need arises.
- **Hydrogen peroxide.**
- **Latex gloves.**
- **Medications.** You're going to want 3 months' supply of any prescription medications you or anyone in your party is currently taking. Bring along a copy of the prescription, so you can have it filled if you have an emergency and you have to leave your bug out location. You're also going to want OTC medications like allergy medicine, pain relievers, cough syrup and any other medications you commonly use.
- **Needle and thread.** Yes, you may have to sew up an open wound.
- **Rubbing Alcohol.**
- **Saline solution.** Used for cleaning wounds and flushing out your eyes.
- **Sawyer venom extractor.** This handy tool will help you extract the venom in the event someone in your party gets bit by a poisonous snake. Make sure you know how to use the extractor ahead of time. You can buy one on Amazon.com for $15.
- **Scissors.**
- **Space blanket.**
- **Stainless steel surgical kit.** You don't want to have to use one of these. You also don't want to

need one, but not have one on hand. Keep a nice, sharp stainless steel kit in your bag just in case you need. It could very easily mean the difference between life and death.

- **Sunblock.**
- **Tape.**
- **Thermometer.**
- **Tweezers.**
- **Various sizes of bandages.**

Food and Utensils

In the chapter on food I recommended you don't buy MREs or freeze-dried food because of the cost. While I don't recommend them for your main food storage, I do recommend them for your bug out bag.

Buy enough freeze-dried food or MREs to last your family for 3 days. You're going to want at least 2 meals a day and you should toss in a few protein bars so you'll be able to have the occasional snack. If you're on the run and moving fast, you're going to burn a lot of calories. If you fail to replace those calories, you're going to slow down and run the risk of burning out before you reach your destination.

Carry as much food as you can practically carry, along with a few tools that will help you get more if you need it. Along with your food, carry fishing line and hooks, so you can catch fish from local streams, rivers and lakes. You should also carry twine and learn how to set traps that will allow you to trap small game animals. A hunting rifle and ammo or a shotgun will allow you to kill game for food.

As far as utensils go, you're going to need a small pot or pan to cook your food in, a small one-burner camping stove and enough fuel to last you for 72-hours. If you're trying to pack light, you can carry a lighter and matches and can build a fire. Just remember, this might be difficult if you have to bug out in the middle of a storm.

If you have babies, don't forget to pack baby food and formula.

Knife

A survival knife will serve you well both in a bug-in situation and as part of your bug out bag.

I suggest buying a good knife and keeping it in your bug out bag. If you end up bugging in, you'll be able to get the knife out of your bag if you need it. Don't remove the knife otherwise, or you run the risk of forgetting to put it away and leaving it at home when you bug out. You don't want to forget your knife. It's one of the most important tools you own.

While it may sound like a neat trick, avoid knives that have hollow compartments in their handles to store stuff. This means the blade doesn't have a full tang, which is the portion of the blade that extends into the handle. A full tang runs the length of the handle and makes for a stronger and better-balanced knife. The blades on the knives with the hidden compartments are more likely to break off when stress is placed on them.

You can buy knives with stainless steel blades or carbon steel blades. Carbon steel holds an edge well, but is more likely to rust and pit when exposed to the elements. Stainless steel is less likely to rust and is tough, but doesn't have the same ability to hold an edge. I prefer the stainless steel and keep a sharpening stone in my BOB to keep the blade on my knife nice and sharp. To be honest with you, I really don't have to sharpen it all that often, so I think it's a fair trade-off to the get the steel that's most capable of withstanding the elements.

A thick-bladed knife that's at least 7 inches in length can be used for most cutting tasks. In a pinch, it can even be used to cut down small trees and chop up firewood. The smaller knives that have flexible blades won't get the job done when it comes to heavier cutting and chopping tasks. Don't go too big or you run the risk of your knife becoming unwieldy. You want a survival knife, not Excalibur.

In addition to your knife, you're going to want a good sheath to carry it in. Make sure you get one that has a strap that locks the knife in tightly. If you have to run or are falling down a hill, you don't want to lose your knife.

KA-BAR

http://www.kabar.com/

If you want a good knife that's been in use since WWII and has withstood the test of time, look no further than the USMC KA-BAR knife. You can get one for $50 and they're practically indestructible. KA-Bar also makes a number of other quality knives for less than $100 and some great higher-end knives if you're looking to spend a bit more for a quality blade.

BUCK Knives

http://www.buckknives.com/

Buck Knives aren't cheap by any stretch of the imagination, but for around a hundred bucks you can get a damn good knife that will withstand the test of time and hold an edge. Check out their line of Survival & Tactical knives for the best Buck has to offer.

SOG
http://www.sogknives.com/outdoor/knives.html

SOG offers a number of good knives that run the gamut from inexpensive to extremely expensive. They carry something for every budget and I've never seen a SOG knife I didn't like.

Kershaw
http://kershaw.kaiusaltd.com/knives/knife/roughneck

The Kershaw Roughneck is a stainless steel knife with a full tang that's sold for less than a hundred bucks. You could spend a lot more and not get as good of a knife. The only downside is it's a little shorter than what I like.

Light

In addition to your crank radio flashlight combo, you're going to want a couple powerful flashlights. You can get decent LED flashlights for less than $20 bucks. Get a couple and don't forget extra bulbs and batteries.

You don't want to get caught out in the woods with no light. Trust me on this one.

You normally wouldn't think of candles as something you'd want to pack in a bug out bag. These aren't your ordinary candles. They're light weight and can be used as a source of light in your tent. They also can be used to provide a bit of warmth on cold nights.

It's also a good idea to carry a few glow sticks. They can provide as much as 12 hours of light per stick and can be used to signal people if you find yourself in need of help.

Maps

It's easy to get turned around, especially if you're trying to sneak off in the middle of the night. Getting lost is never fun, but it can be fatal in a bug out situation.

You're going to want to have road maps of your local area and the area you're bugging out to, along with a topographical map of your bug out area. Don't assume a handheld GPS is going to be enough. You can pack one if you'd like, but it shouldn't be your only means of navigation. If you lose the signal or your batteries run, you're going to end up completely lost in no time.

Money

You never know when you're going to need some cash on hand. You may need to bribe someone to get past a roadblock or you might just need some extra cash for bridge toll. I know we're trying to prep on a budget, but if you have anything in savings, you might want to pull a couple hundred dollars out and toss it in your bug out bag.

Money talks and you might find yourself in a situation in which you're unable to withdraw money from an ATM or use your card. If this happens, the only currency you're going to have is the cash you have on hand. You don't want to end up dead broke and without any options.

Multitool

You're going to want to have a multitool around.

These handy tools contain a number of useful tools in a small package. I've seen multitools that contain knives, pliers, wire strippers, bottle openers, screwdrivers, saws, files and all sorts of other tools.

The tried and true Leatherman is probably your best bet, but Gerber makes a line of less expensive multitools that seem to hold up pretty well.

Radio and Cell Phone

It's a good idea to keep a small radio with you that you can use to keep up to date with current events. Even if you're bugging out to a location where you won't get a signal, you may at some point want to sneak back close enough to civilization to find out how things are going. A handheld radio will allow you to keep abreast of current events without having to make contact with other potentially hostile human beings.

You're also going to want a cell phone, so you can at some point try to get in touch with loved ones. Again, you may have to head to higher ground or sneak back closer to civilization to use your phone.

I prefer the hand-crank type of radio because they don't need batteries. All you have to do is turn the crank for a minute or two and you get up to a half hour's charge on your radio. You can find hand-crank radios now that charge your cell phone and work as flashlights. How's that for multitasking?

Paracord

My favorite way to pack paracord is in the form of a paracord survival belt. You can buy one for $20 to $50, or you can make your own using the instructions at the link below:

http://www.instructables.com/id/How-to-make-a-Paracord-Rescue-Belt/

These belts can be used to keep your pants up until you find yourself in need of paracord, at which time you unravel the belt to access upwards of 50 feet of cord. If each person in your party wears one of these belts, you'll have a lot of cord. Just be sure to save 3 feet or so to keep your pants up.

There are a ton of uses for paracord. Here are some of the more common uses:

- Bind a person's hands and feet together.
- Create a hammock.
- Create a pulley system to move heavy objects.
- Create snares to trap game animals.
- Lash stuff together.
- Lift your food up off the ground, so bears, raccoons and other animals can't get to it.

- Makeshift tourniquet. Use a stick and some paracord to create a tourniquet that can be used to stop bleeding.
- Set up traps and trip wires.
- Shoe laces.
- String it between trees and use it as a clothes line.
- The internal strands can be used as fishing line. The cord can be strung through the gills of fish to create a makeshift stringer.
- Tie hooks off to it and use it as a trot line.
- Tie it to sticks to create a splint for broken bones.
- Tie stuff down.
- Tie stuff to your backpack, so you won't have to carry it.
- Tie yourself to the others in your group when hiking to ensure no one gets lost.
- Unravel the cord to get at the internal strands, which can be used as thread to sew up clothing.
- Use it as a leash to tie off pets or other animals.

Paracord bracelets are also available, but they don't have enough paracord for my tastes.

Pet Supplies

If you're planning on bringing your pets along when you bug out, you're going to need pet care supplies. Make sure you pack a leash, food and any medications your pet needs. You also need to make sure each of your pets has a tag with your contact information on it in case they get separated from the group.

Shelter

When it comes to shelter, there are two general schools of thought.

Some survivalists will pack a couple tarps and call it a day. They'll use tree branches to create a makeshift tent and will place rocks around the edges of the tarp to hold it in place. One tarp is used to make the tent, while the other is used as ground cover in order to stay dry and insulate the sleeping area a bit. This is by the far the cheapest option. All you need to buy is the two tarps and a hatchet to cut down the branches.

While this method is inexpensive, it can be extremely uncomfortable and potentially fatal if the outside temperatures creep low enough. You'd better make sure you have a dang good sleeping bag if you decide to go this route.

I recommend trying it in your backyard for a couple days in the middle of winter to see just how uncomfortable it can be. With only a tarp between you and the elements, you can feel pretty exposed, especially if a cold breeze finds its way into your makeshift tent. Bugs and things that slither and crawl around in the night can also be a huge problem.

Unless you're a survivalist of the highest order, I recommend a lightweight tent. The size and weight of the tent will depend on how many people you need to sleep in it.

If you're only planning on sleeping a couple people in the tent, a pup tent is an inexpensive option. You can get pup tents for less than $50 that are both durable and able to withstand the elements. You'll have to pay more for bigger tents. You're going to want to buy as light of a tent as you can afford or you run the risk of adding serious weight to your bug out bag. You can find pup tents on Ebay for less than $20.

Steer clear of the family style tents that are big enough to accommodate entire parties of people. These tents are heavy and are a pain in the butt to set up. You want to be able to set up and take down in a hurry if need be and you won't be able to do that with a huge tent.

Don't worry about buying the top-of-the line ultra-light trekking tents, unless that's what you really want. You can get a good tent that's relatively lightweight for a lot less than the $500or more the ultra-lights will set you back. You can get a good backpacking tent for around a couple hundred bucks if you catch the right sale.

Here are a few sites to watch for good deals. Keep an eye on their closeout and end-of-season sales to get the best prices.

Dick's Sporting Goods
http://www.dickssportinggoods.com

Dick's carries a number of good backpacking tents and has something for every budget. Watch for 20% off site-wide sales to net huge online savings. If you have a Dick's close to home, keep an eye out in their stores for end-season clearance sales. I've found items marked down as much as 60% off the normal price when Dick's decides it's time to clear them out.

Backside All-Season Tents

http://www.trailtents.com/site/1412894/page/872275

Backside offers a number of lightweight backpacking tent for decent prices. You can get one-, two- or three-man tents from the link above.

Coleman

http://www.coleman.com/product/hooliganreg-3-tent/2000012431?contextCategory=11070

While I wouldn't recommend their more expensive backpacking tents because you can get more bang for your buck from other manufacturers, their Hooligan 4-man backpacking tent is a decent deal at just under a hundred bucks. It's capable of handling most conditions and is a good choice for a family on a serious budget. There are better tents out there, but not at this price.

North Face

http://www.thenorthface.com/catalog/sc-gear/equipment-tents.html

When most people think of North Face gear, they see dollar signs. It's true that some of the North Face gear is expensive, but they also have a handful of tents for sale that are under $250. One of my personal favorites is the Rock 22, which is a two-man tent that costs just over $200.

Eureka

http://store.eurekatent.com/backpacking-tents

Eureka offers a number of backpacking tents that cost between $100 and $200. A good choice if you're planning on flying solo is their Solitaire tent. It weighs in at less than 5 pounds and will cost you less than a hundred bucks. Now that's a pretty good deal! Their Spitfire line will cost you a little more, but they also weigh less than 5 pounds.

Sleeping Bag

You're going to want a sleeping bag that's light and capable of keeping you warm in the harshest conditions you might face. If you're planning on bugging out to an area that rarely reach 20 degrees F, you're not going to need as robust of a sleeping bag as you will if you're planning on bugging out to an area where the temperature drops below zero and stays there for months on end.

The cost of your sleeping bag is going to depend on how cold of weather you're going to need it to shield you against. You can get good sleeping bags from both North Face and Eureka. You can get to their websites from the links in the previous section.

I'm a big fan of the Sierra Designs sleeping bags, but they aren't exactly cheap.

A -20 degree bag will cost you nearly $700. This bag will be capable of keeping you alive in temperatures as low as -20 degrees F. You can get a 20 degree bag for $120.

This bag will keep you warm until the temperatures drop below 20 degrees F. Here's a link to Sierra Designs sleeping bags:

https://www.sierradesigns.com/c-26-sleeping-bags.aspx

Toiletries

You're going to want the following toiletries in your bug out bag:

- A toothbrush.
- Toothpaste.
- Deodorant.
- Toilet paper.
- Tampons or maxi pads.
- A razor.
- A bar of soap.

Tools

There are a few tools you're going to want in your bug out bag. Here are the tools everyone should have in their bag:

- A camp shovel.
- A folding saw.
- A lock pick kit. Make sure owning one of these kits is legal in your area. You also need to make sure you know how to use it. You never know when you'll need to pick a lock.

- A pry bar.
- A small firearm cleaning and lubing kit.
- A small hatchet.
- A wrench.
- Duct tape.
- Electrical tape.
- Flare gun and flares.
- Gloves.
- Hand torch.
- Ice pick.
- Kerosene heater and fuel.
- Needlenose pliers.
- Sandpaper.
- Super glue.
- Wire strippers.

Start with these tools and add anything else you feel you need to add. When it comes to tools, there's no need to buy them new. You can find everything you need at garage sales and flea markets for a couple bucks a piece. The only thing you might have to buy new is the lock pick kit.

<u>**Water**</u>

When you bug out, you may end up traveling on foot in hot weather. I've seen people recommend a couple liters of water per person per day. I recommend as much water as you can carry, with the minimum amount being a gallon per person.

The problem with carrying a lot of water is the weight. Water is heavy and can really weigh down your bug out bag. If you're bugging out to an area that has a lot of water, you can bring water purification tablets and filters instead of packing a bunch of water. I still recommend packing as much water as you can because you never know when you might have to strike out to a different location that may have less water.

You can buy water filtration straws that allow you to drink directly from most water sources. They don't filter out everything, but do get rid of nasty stuff like giardia and a number of other pathogens. It wouldn't hurt to toss a couple of these lightweight straws into your bag. You can find them for less than a ten-spot each if you look around.

You're going to need something to store clean water in if you find it. You can use a good, old-fashioned canteen that you can clip to the outside of your bag or you can go with an internal water storage system like the CamelBak. CamelBak sells backpacks with their hydration system built into them, but they tend to be a bit on the expensive side. The larger CamelBak bags that would be best-suited for bug out bags will run you $200 to $300.

Ways to Make Fire

You're going to want multiple ways to make fire.

The first two items you're going to want are waterproof matches and a few butane torches, along with a bottle (or two) of fluid for the torches. This is going to be your easiest way to make fire, as long as your torches are working and you have fluid for the torches.

It's a good idea to have a couple other ways to make fire just in case.

A flint and a scraper will allow you create sparks that can be directed toward tender to create a fire. The scrapers sold today can be struck thousands of times and only cost around $10. You're going to want to have a couple of these in your bag.

You should also keep a couple 9-volt batteries and some steel wool in your bag. Touch the steel wool to both terminals on the battery and it will catch on fire. You can do this with other types of batteries as well, but it's easier with 9-volt batteries.

Whistle

This inexpensive addition to your bug out bag can be used to alert others to your position if you get lost. Each member of your party should have a whistle they wear around their neck, so they'll have it at the ready in case it's needed.

The Get Home Bag

There's a little problem with having a bug out bag that you keep at home. What happens if disaster strikes while you're outside the home? What do you do then? Whenever possible, you head home, either to bug in or to grab your gear and bug out.

A Get Home Bag can be kept in your vehicle to help up your odds of making it home safely to your family and your gear. This is a bag you fill with the gear you need to get home safely. It's similar to a bug out bag, in that it's a survival bag packed with the gear you're going to need to survive. It's different in that you aren't going to need to pack everything you need to survive for 72 hours. You just need enough gear to get you home.

You don't need a big bag. In most cases, a daypack will suffice. You're going to want something durable and light because you might have to travel a significant distance by foot. If you have and extra backpack laying around, you can save some money by using it as your get home bag. If you do decide to buy one, go for something plain that isn't going to draw attention. You want a regular looking backpack that's a neutral color like black, green or brown—not something bright enough to call attention to yourself. While you might think urban camo is a good idea, this will look out of place in the city and may draw unwanted attention.

Your bag doesn't have to be big and bulky. In fact, the lighter it is, the better. You're going to want to be able to make good time on foot if you have to walk home. Your goal is making it home in the shortest amount of time possible, not surviving for days on end. Most of your gear should be in your BOB, not your Get Home Bag.

You're going to want the following gear in your Get Home Bag:

- An emergency blanket.
- A map. If the normal route you take home is blocked, you're going to have to figure out an alternate route. A map will allow you to choose the fastest route.
- A spare phone.
- Bandana.
- Batteries.
- Cash.
- Duct tape. Can be used for a number of purposes, from emergency repair to taping up wounds.
- Flashlight.
- A couple days' worth of any medications you need to take.
- Multitool.
- Paracord.
- Pry bar. You may have to break locks and pry open doors. A small pry bar can be a lifesaver in an emergency situation.
- Raincoat.
- Scissors.
- Small first aid kit.
- Small radio.

- Snacks. You don't need a lot of food, just enough to stave off hunger and keep your stomach from rumbling.
- Solar charger for your cell phone.
- Spare keys.
- Toilet paper.
- Walking shoes.
- Water. Carry a few bottles of water in your bag.
- Whistle.

Remember, the whole goal of this bag is to get you home to your family and the rest of your supplies. You want to pack light, but still pack the items you're most likely to need.

Your Bug Out Location

You're going to need a location you can bug out to in the event you need to get off the grid. This location needs to be off the beaten path in an area where it isn't likely to be found. Ideally, you're going to want to have some sort of structure at your bug out location that you can use as a rally point—and a home base, if need be.

The ideal location will be far enough away from your current location that it won't be affected by the same disaster, but close enough that you can get to it without having to travel across the country. I see preppers buying up land thousands of miles away from where they live because it's inexpensive. The problem with this line of thinking is you have to travel by vehicle to get to your bug out location. What happens if vehicle travel is restricted or state lines are blocked off?

If you can find cheap property in the middle of nowhere, you can buy it and build a bug out shelter on your property. A tiny shelter with a bed or two and room to store your supplies will be sufficient. Some people buy an inexpensive camp trailer and park it on their property. Some people even bury cargo containers in the earth, so their bug out location is hidden from prying eyes.

As long as you have a relatively secure location, you're going to want to stockpile similar stuff to what you have at home in your bug out location. If you have to bug out quickly, you may have to leave your cache at home. Having an additional cache at your bug out location will ensure you're outfitted no matter where you end up. If you only have supplies at home and end up having to bug out, you're only going to have the supplies in your bug out bag.

Your BOB is intended to get you to your location within 72 hours. It isn't designed to help you survive once you get there.

Make sure you check in on your stockpile at your bug out location frequently. If you've chosen a good location, it will be off the beaten path, but there's always the chance someone will stumble across it and help themselves to your stuff. It's better to find this out ahead of time, as opposed to finding out when you bug out.

Keeping Your Cache Safe

So you've spent countless hours finding the best deals and have built up a huge stockpile of food and supplies. You've created a bug out bag, identified multiple locations you can bug out to in the event there's an emergency and are fully prepared for most emergency situations. What do you do next?

Well, for all too many preppers, the answer is they brag about it to anyone who will listen. Friends, family members, coworkers, acquaintances on Facebook. You're ready and want the whole world to know how prepared you are.

There's just one problem.

You're telling people who know who you are and where you live that you have food and supplies stockpiled. When an emergency hits, the people who didn't prepare for themselves are sure to come calling. They'll either come to you begging for handouts—or they'll come armed and ready to take what you have. People you thought were your friends might not be so friendly when you turn them away from what they thought was going to be a free meal and a place to stay.

You shouldn't tell anyone about your prepping unless you're prepared to support them when they come calling. Sure, you may love your family and wish the best for them, but do you really want your Aunt and Uncle to show up with their 4 kids when disaster strikes? Not only will your house be crowded; your 6 month supply of food just became a one month supply.

When you announce your stockpile to the world, you also open yourself up to thieves who watch social media sites for people announcing they have items of value. Thieves know preppers usually have valuable items like generators, tools and firearms, amongst other things. They stake out your house and watch and wait until you leave, then your gear becomes theirs and you're back where you started—with nothing.

All this could be avoided by being extremely selective about who you speak to about your prepping. In addition to not telling people about your cache, you should have an alarm system installed in your house. Yes, it costs money, but it could be the difference between a thief breaking a window and being deterred from robbing your house when the alarm goes off and you losing everything.

Make sure your kids know they need to keep your gear a secret. It's going to be tough to keep young kids quiet, but older children should be able to understand that the safety of the family is at risk if they tell people about the items you have stockpiled.

Defending Your Cache

Depending on the disaster that strikes, there could be roving packs of criminals or desperate people out looking for shelter and supplies. These people are going to be armed and there's a good chance they're going to have guns.

I know there are people who are morally opposed to owning firearms, especially in the wake of recent tragedies. I don't force my views on anyone, but I will tell you this. In a lawless situation, the people who have firearms are going to be much safer than the people who don't. If you aren't armed, your only recourse when armed thugs come around will be to hide and hope you aren't found. If you are found, you're going to lose your supplies, your shelter and possibly your life.

Would you be able to live with yourself if the women in your party were kidnapped by a gang of armed street thugs? If you're opposed to owning firearms, you can skip this chapter. Just know that you'd better be dang good at hiding both your gear and yourself.

I recommend owning at least 3 guns and an ample supply of ammo for each of your weapons. A gun without ammo is nothing more than a club. It might look scary, but you'll soon be found out if you aren't able to shoot back.

The first gun you should purchase is a good rifle.

A rifle can serve multiple purposes. It can be used for both hunting game and self-defense. The problem is rifles aren't very concealable. If you find yourself in a situation where you don't want the world to know you're armed, you're going to have a tough time concealing a rifle.

The second gun you should get is a handgun.

The caliber you get is up to you, but be aware the ammo for higher caliber weapons is more expensive, so it's going to cost you a lot more to stockpile. My personal preference is a .40 caliber handgun because it gives a good balance between cost of ammo and firepower. A 9mm is also a good choice, but some say it's underpowered. I will tell you this. There isn't a person on this planet who will agree to let you shoot them center of mass with a 9mm round unless they have a death wish. A 9 is a good choice for the women and teenagers in your party if you plan on arming them.

The last weapon I recommend is a shotgun. It can be used for close-quarters combat and is one of the few weapons that don't require good aim to hit your target. All you have to do is point and shoot. Shotgun shells contain a number of projectiles that spread out to cover a large area as they travel downrange. There are also slugs available that are essentially chunks of lead that hit hard and do maximum damage. In addition to self-defense, shotguns can be used to hunt small game and birds.

If you want to add a fourth weapon to your cache, a .22 rifle is a great choice. It isn't ideal for self-defense because the rounds aren't all that powerful, but it is a good choice for hunting small or even medium sized game. The ammo is extremely cheap. You can pick up 500 round boxes for less than $20.

Once you buy a firearm, you need to practice with it until you're comfortable using it. Be sure to practice shooting while moving, because emergency situations in which you have time to stand still and carefully aim are few and far between.

You're also going to want to make sure you're comfortable taking your gun apart and reassembling it for cleaning and maintenance. A clean, well-oiled gun is less likely to misfire or jam.

If you can legally obtain one in your state, a Concealed Carry Weapons Permit is a good idea. A CCW allows you to carry a concealed gun on your person when you're out and about. This will not only allow you to stay safe in an emergency, it'll keep you safe in your daily life.

Firearms aren't cheap by any stretch of the imaginations, but you can find pretty good deals if you look in the right places.

Shop around and check sites like GunBroker.com to see what's for sale. You might stumble across someone selling a nice gun for an amazingly low price. If you take your time and watch auction sites that sell guns, you can get used guns for half of what they'd cost new.

Pawn shops are another place that sells guns at a steep discount.

When a pawn shop quotes you a high price, come back at them with an offer that's lower than what you want to pay. Chances are, the owner of the shop will be willing to meet you somewhere in the middle and will give you a good deal on the gun. They don't pay a lot for the guns that come into their shops, and they're happy as long as they sell them for a profit.

You can get good deals at gun shows, too. Walk around the show before you buy anything to get an idea of the going rate for some of the guns being sold. Always try to get a lower price than what you're quoted. The worst that can happen is you're told no.

Contact Me

I hope you enjoyed the book and gained helpful knowledge from it. If you liked what you read, I'd really appreciate a positive review. Thanks in advance!

If you have any questions or concerns, feel free to drop me a line at the following e-mail address:

miklanderson2@yahoo.com